Comportamiento y modales en la **biblioteca**

Manners in the **Library**

¡Así debemos ser!
Way to Be!

por/by Carrie Finn   ilustrado por/illustrated by Chris Lensch

Nuestro agradecimiento especial a nuestros asesores por su experiencia/Special thanks to our advisers for their expertise:

Kay Augustine, Directora Asociada/Associate Director
Instituto para el Desarrollo del Carácter de la Universidad Drake/
Institute for Character Development at Drake University

Susan Kesselring, M.A., Educadora de Alfabetismo/Literacy Educator
Distrito Escolar Rosemount–Apple Valley–Eagan (Minnesota)/
Rosemount–Apple Valley–Eagan School District (Minnesota)

PICTURE WINDOW BOOKS
a capstone imprint

Editor: Shelly Lyons
Translation Services: Strictly Spanish
Designer: Eric Manske
Production Specialist: Sarah Bennett
Art Director: Nathan Gassman
Editorial Director: Nick Healy
The illustrations in this book were created digitally.

Picture Window Books
A Capstone Imprint
151 Good Counsel Drive
P.O. Box 669
Mankato, MN 56002-0669
877-845-8392
www.capstonepub.com

All books published by Picture Window Books
are manufactured with paper containing at least
10 percent post-consumer waste.

Library of Congress Cataloging-in-Publication Data
Finn, Carrie.
[Manners in the library. Spanish & English]
Comportamiento y modales en la biblioteca / por Carrie Finn ; ilustrado
por Chris Lensch = Manners in the library / by Carrie Finn ; illustrated by
Chris Lensch.
p. cm.—(¡Así debemos ser! = Way to be!)
Summary: "Explains many different ways that children can show manners in
the library—in both English and Spanish"—Provided by publisher.
Includes index.
ISBN 978-1-4048-6697-3 (library binding)
1. Library etiquette—Juvenile literature. 2. Etiquette for children and
teenagers. I. Lensch, Chris. II. Title: Manners in the library. III. Series.
Z716.43.F5618 2011
395.5'3—dc22   2010041030

Printed in the United States of America in North Mankato, Minnesota.
092010   005933CGS11

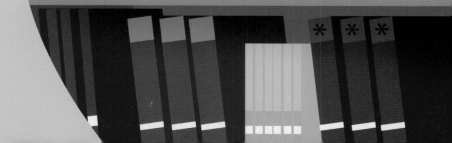

Good manners are an important part of any library visit. Lots of different people use the library in lots of different ways. By using good manners, you can show respect for everyone.

There are many ways you can use good manners in the library.

Comportarse bien y tener buenos modales son una parte importante de cualquier visita a la biblioteca. Muchas personas usan la biblioteca de muchas maneras diferentes. Comportándote bien y teniendo buenos modales, tú puedes demostrar respeto por todos.

Hay muchas maneras de comportarse bien y tener buenos modales en la biblioteca.

Mia uses her inside voice in the library. She keeps

quiet so she won't disturb other people.

She is using good manners.

Mia habla bien bajo en la biblioteca. Ella no hace

ruido para no molestar a las otras personas.

Ella se comporta bien.

Charles wants to find a book on dinosaurs. He says "Please" when he asks a librarian for help. **He is using good manners.**

Charles quiere pedir un libro acerca de dinosaurios. Él dice "Por favor" cuando le pide ayuda al bibliotecario. **Él tiene buenos modales.**

Kyle is hungry, but he saves his apple until he leaves the library.

He is using good manners.

Kyle tiene hambre, pero él guarda su manzana hasta que sale de la biblioteca.

Él se comporta bien.

Ruth helps her little sister find a sing-along video. They are careful with the videos, books, and computers in the library. **They are using good manners.**

Ruth ayuda a su hermana pequeña a buscar un video de canciones. Ellas son cuidadosas con los videos, libros y computadoras en la biblioteca. **Ellas tienen buenos modales.**

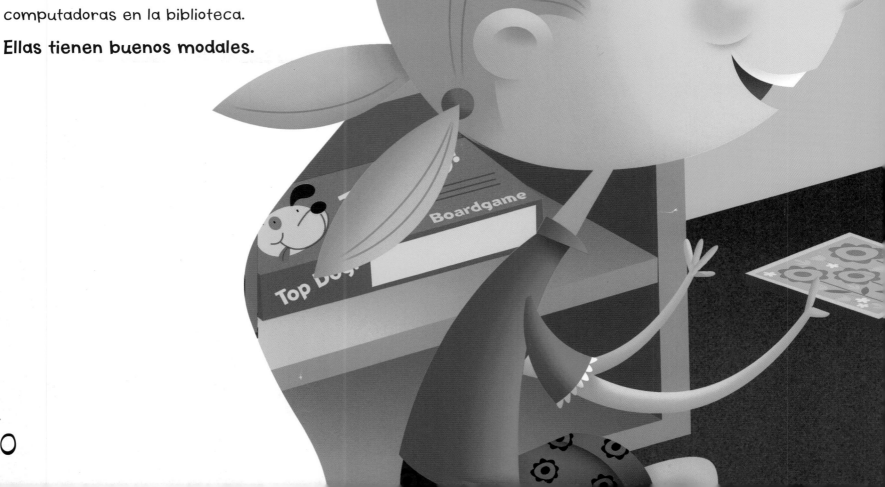

Grace loves to learn about lions. Still, she checks out only the number of books she knows she'll read.

She is using good manners.

A Grace le encanta aprender acerca de leones. Pero ella sólo pide el número de libros que sabe que leerá.

Ella se comporta bien.

13

Mary spends a rainy day in the library.

She reads silently to herself so she

doesn't bother other people.

She is using good manners.

Mary pasa un día lluvioso en la biblioteca.

Ella lee en silencio para no molestar

a los demás.

Ella tiene buenos modales.

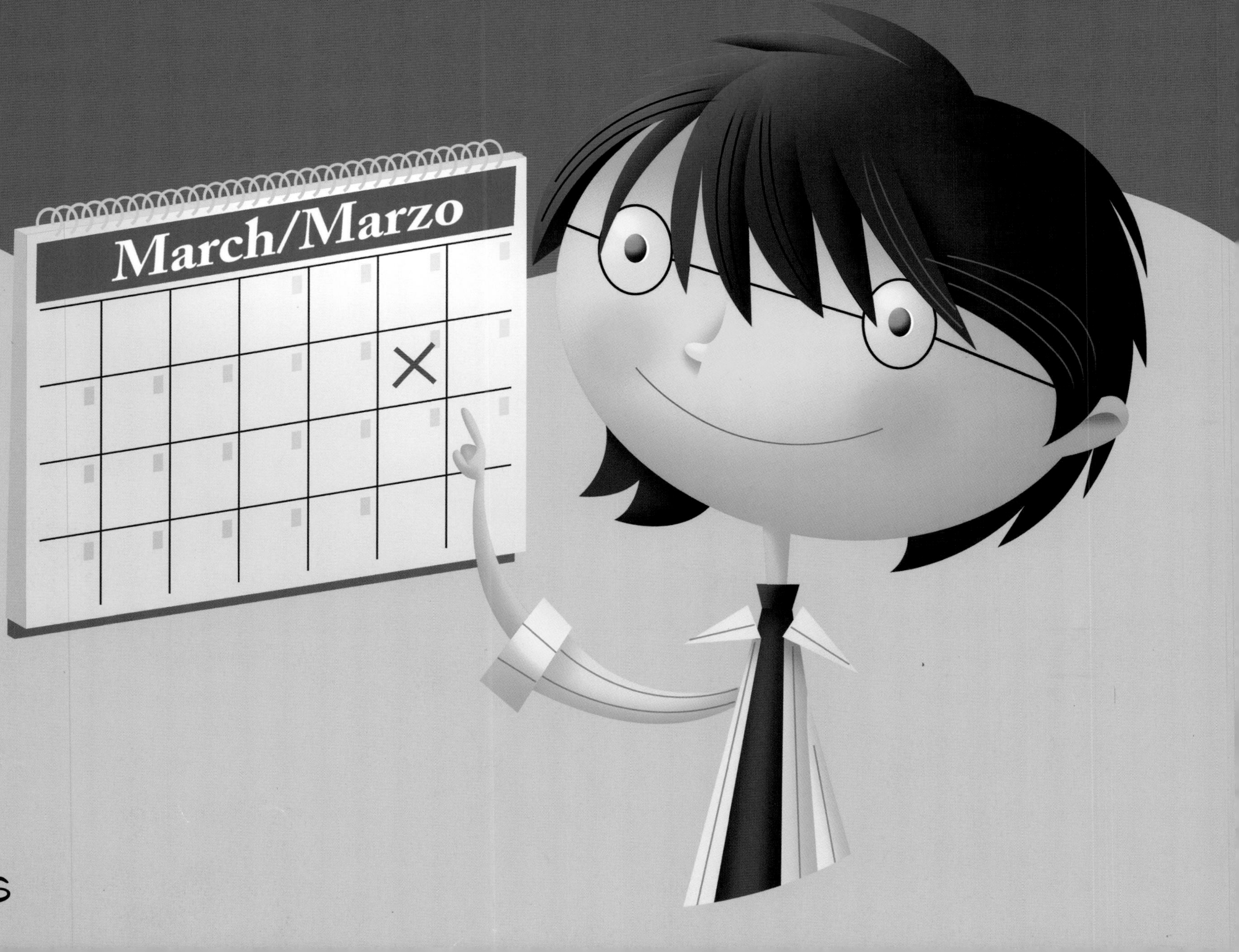
March/Marzo

Mark's books are due on Friday.

He returns his books on time.

He is using good manners.

Los libros de Mark vencen el viernes.

Él los devuelve a su debido tiempo.

Él se comporta bien.

17

During story time, Joey and Tonya
sit quietly and listen.
They are using good manners.

Mientras el maestro lee un cuento, Joey
y Tonya escuchan sentados en silencio.
Ellos tienen buenos modales.

19

Manny does not interrupt his mom
while she reads to his little brother.
He is using good manners.

Manny no interrumpe a su mamá
mientras ella le lee a su hermanito.
Él tiene buenos modales.

You can learn a lot at the library. You can also have fun. By using good manners, you can make sure everyone else enjoys his or her visit, too.

Tú puedes aprender muchas cosas en la biblioteca. Tú también puedes divertirte. Teniendo buenos modales y comportándote bien, puedes asegurar que todos los demás también disfruten su visita.

Fun Facts/
Datos divertidos

There are more than 117,000 libraries in the United States.

Hay más de 117,000 bibliotecas en Estados Unidos.

Mexico is home to the oldest library in North America.

La biblioteca más antigua de América del Norte se encuentra en México.

The Library of Congress has the most books of any library in the United States.

La Biblioteca del Congreso tiene más libros que cualquier biblioteca en Estados Unidos.

Internet Sites

FactHound offers a safe, fun way to find Internet sites related to this book. All of the sites on FactHound have been researched by our staff.

Here's all you do:

Visit www.facthound.com

Type in this code: 9781404866973

Super-cool stuff! Check out projects, games and lots more at www.capstonekids.com

Index

Sitios de Internet

FactHound brinda una forma segura y divertida de encontrar sitios de Internet relacionados con este libro. Todos los sitios en FactHound han sido investigados por nuestro personal.

Esto es todo lo que tienes que hacer:

Visita www.facthound.com

Ingresa este código: 9781404866973

¡Algo súper divertido! Hay proyectos, juegos y mucho más en www.capstonekids.com

Índice

24